Other books by Graham Greene

* *British title*

The Return of
A. J. Raffles

An Edwardian Comedy in Three Acts
based somewhat loosely on
E. W. Hornung's characters in
The Amateur Cracksman

Graham Greene

SIMON AND SCHUSTER
NEW YORK

Published by Simon and Schuster
A Gulf+Western Company
Rockefeller Center, 630 Fifth Avenue
New York, New York 10020
Designed by Edith Fowler
Manufactured in the United States of America
1   2   3   4   5   6   7   8   9   10

Library of Congress Cataloging in Publication Data

Greene, Graham, date.
    The return of A. J. Raffles.

    I. Hornung, Ernest William, 1866–1921.   The
amateur cracksman.   II. Title.
PR6013.R44R4   822'.9'12   76-228
ISBN 0-671-22297-X

Application for professional performance
of the play in the United States and Canada
should be made to:
Monica McCall
International Creative Management, Inc.
40 West 57th Street
New York, New York 10019

In France application should be made to:
Bureau Littéraire D. Clairouin
66 Rue de Miromesnil
Paris 8ème

In all other parts of the world
application should be made to:
Dr. Jan van Loewen Ltd.
International Copyright Agency
81–83 Shaftesbury Avenue
London W1V8BX

Author's Note

This story cannot of course be accepted as strictly true to history. I have in one respect seriously deviated from the truth—the Marquess of Queensberry met his end in January 1900 and I have extended his life into the late summer of that year. It is very questionable too whether the Prince of Wales would have been on terms of friendship with the Marquess, and I have no evidence that the Marquess had a country house in Hertfordshire.

On the other hand the gold box presented by the theatrical profession to the Prince of Wales is in no way fictitious, nor are the difficulties the Prince had with foreign uniforms. And I am prepared to defend the truth of Raffles' return from South Africa alive. His chronicler, and his close companion, Bunny, wrote a moving account of Raffles' death and claimed to have been beside him when he was "killed," but Bunny had every reason for falsifying history, to disguise the fact that, far from being in South Africa, he was, at the date of Spion Kop, incarcerated in Reading Gaol, where he had the good fortune to meet Oscar Wilde.

GRAHAM GREENE

Characters

(*not* in order of appearance)

A. J. Raffles
Bunny
Lord Alfred Douglas
"Mr. Portland"
Inspector Mackenzie
The Marquess of Queensberry
A Lady called Alice
A lady's maid called Mary
Mr. Smith, head porter of Albany
Captain von Blixen

ACT I

Raffles' old chambers in Albany, Piccadilly,
late summer of 1900.

ACT II

The Marquess of Queensberry's bedroom in his
country house in Hertfordshire a few nights later.

ACT III

Raffles' chambers in Albany
early the next morning.

Act I

The date is the late summer of 1900, a few months before the death of the old Queen. The scene a set of chambers in Albany, which was once described by Conan Doyle as an "aristocratic rookery." Even if we did not know it was Albany, where at that date no woman, cat or dog was allowed to reside, we would recognise a bachelor's apartment: the rather heavy furniture, the comfortable leather armchairs, the photograph on the desk of an elderly woman—a rather obvious mother—on the back wall the photograph of a cricket team, and hanging on either side of it a cricket bat on which the signatures of a team have been inscribed, and a red leather cricket ball dangling in a net from a nail. Below them a large chest with a flat top like a cabin trunk. Hornung has described the room when Raffles occupied it: "That dear den of disorder in good taste, with a carved bookcase, the dresser and chests of still older oak, and the Watts and Rossettis hung anyhow on the walls." A man in his early thirties in full evening dress is moving restlessly round the room, sometimes consulting his watch. He is good-looking in a rather weak way with depraved aristocratic features. On the right a door into the hall stands open, curtains are drawn over the windows on the left, and in the back wall a door leads to a bedroom. The young man knocks impatiently at this door.

LORD ALFRED: Bunny! Bunny! For God's sake hurry up. The curtain at Covent Garden won't stay down for us. I asked Stephen to meet us first at the Criterion. Drinking brandy and selzer too fast always gives me the hiccups. One mustn't have hiccups at *Carmen*—too middle-class.

> *He tries the handle of the door, but the door is locked.*

Let me in, Bunny. Why lock the door? You needn't be so careful of your precious virtue. I like a bit of flesh and prison benches make for hard bottoms.

> *Lord Alfred goes to the wall and unhooks the cricket bat, then he takes the ball out of the net, arranges it carefully like a golf ball and strikes it at the door.*

LORD ALFRED: A goal! A goal! If that's the right term.

> *The door is quickly opened and Bunny, a small thin young man in his early thirties, comes furiously into the room. He is in his evening shirt sleeves, with his white tie dangling unfastened. His hair is cut very short.*

BUNNY: How dare you, Bosie. Put the bat back.

LORD ALFRED: (*obeying*) A sacred relic. Do people always write on these things?

BUNNY: Of course not. That was Raffles' bat in the last Test he played in. He made 105 not out against Australia and won us the Ashes.

LORD ALFRED: Ashes? How very morbid. But, Bunny, we *must* be off. Poor Stephen will think we've gone without him.

BUNNY: I can't tie this wretched tie.

LORD ALFRED: Turn round. I'll tie it for you.

BUNNY: I was never very good at it. Raffles always had to help me. And one forgets things after two years' picking oakum in prison.

LORD ALFRED: Chokie Oscar always calls it. He's forgotten nothing—except his friends. Now that's a very fine bow, Bunny. Raffles couldn't have done better. (*With a caress of his fingers*) I must admit the back of your neck has a certain epicene charm, but I wish your hair would grow faster. It has a distinctly penal look. All right for the gallery, of course, but unusual in a box. And very noticeable I would say at the Criterion.

BUNNY: I've no intention of going to the Criterion. I don't like Stephen. He was very offensive to me last week. He said his valet had known me at Reading. I hadn't even exchanged whispers with him in the exercise yard. I shall go direct from here, Bosie, to your box.

LORD ALFRED: Stephen is rather highly-coloured, but I thought he might cheer you up after all the greyness of gaol.

He tosses up the cricket ball and fails to catch it.

Butterfingers! Unlike your Raffles I was never any good at outdoor games. So much depends on the boring weather the English like to talk about. But in a bedroom . . . rain or snow, sun or showers . . . who cares? Are you always faithful to your Raffles?

BUNNY: Always. He was a great man, Bosie, and he died a hero's death at Spion Kop. I'll be ready in a moment.

Bunny goes to fetch his tails while Lord Alfred prowls around the room. He pauses by the photograph of the cricket team and calls out to Bunny in the bedroom.

LORD ALFRED: And this photograph? Which of the flannelled fools is Raffles?

BUNNY: (*returning and putting on his tails*) You wouldn't have called him a fool if you'd faced him as he came up to bowl. He's there on the left of the captain. It's the Gentlemen's team against the Players in '94. They hadn't yet learned that he could bat just as well as he could bowl.

LORD ALFRED: And the gentleman with the enormous beard on the captain's right?

BUNNY: Don't pretend you don't know that fellow W. G. Grace?

LORD ALFRED: So Raffles could bowl as well as he could bat? Was he bisexual too, Bunny?

BUNNY: Of course not. He never looked twice at a woman. If you want to meet Stephen you'd better be off. I'll meet you in the box.

LORD ALFRED: Bunny, whatever have you got around your sleeve?

Bunny is wearing a black armlet.

BUNNY: It's only six months since the Boers killed him, Bosie.

LORD ALFRED: You can't possibly go to Covent Garden wearing that. Take it off at once. They'll think the Queen has died. It would be a bit exaggerated even then.

BUNNY: Can't I mourn him for six months? You don't know all the things he did for me.

LORD ALFRED: I know what you told Oscar in Reading Gaol—that Raffles escaped to the war and left you to carry the blame.

BUNNY: I know I told Wilde that. I was bitter at first, but it was all my own fault I was caught. Raffles was right to escape. He wouldn't have got off with a two-year sentence. That old monster Mackenzie of Scotland Yard had been on his trail for years. I was only small game. Why, Mackenzie even spoke up for me at the trial. I can see him now, the old greybeard, in his heavy musty tweeds. His nose was always running. He said I had a weak character and I had been seduced by an archcriminal. He said it in a self-righteous Scotch accent which made it worse.

LORD ALFRED: Seduced, Bunny?

BUNNY: He only meant mentally. Why aren't you off to your highly-coloured friend Stephen, Bosie?

LORD ALFRED: I can't go with you to Covent Garden if you are wearing that thing. But for you I'll give up the Criterion. Stephen is beginning to bore me. He has developed a hideous taste for pink champagne. It makes me think he has secret connexions with women. I begin to love you, Bunny. No, no, don't moue at me. Like a brother of course. Ever since Oscar went to chokie I've discovered a strong interest in the criminal classes. Wouldn't you sometimes like to return to a life of crime?

BUNNY: There'd be no fun in it without Raffles. And no future. In a tight spot I always knew he was there. Do you know, I really believe he chose to die at Spion Kop to help me in the only way he could? He couldn't spring me from prison, but he made his will the night before he was killed. They found it on his body stained with blood. He left me everything. These chambers and everything in them.

LORD ALFRED: Including the bat and ball. What do you keep in this old chest? The Crown Jewels?

BUNNY: The last things Raffles stole.

LORD ALFRED: Show me.

Bunny opens the chest and Lord Alfred peers inside.

LORD ALFRED: It's empty.

Bunny releases a catch and a false top falls from the lid, making a tray which he lifts out and places on top of the chest.

LORD ALFRED: A lot of old junk.

BUNNY: They are the Raffles Relics from the Black Museum at Scotland Yard.

LORD ALFRED: How did he get them?

BUNNY: You'll never get to Covent Garden if I begin to tell you that. They were labelled Relics of an Amateur Cracks·man. They could never pin anything on him. He got them from under the nose of Inspector Mackenzie himself.

Bunny lifts out the relics one by one for inspection.

BUNNY: His revolver. He never fired it. He only used it to frighten. Here's a life preserver. There's blood on that. Raffles was ashamed of that blow, but it saved me from prison. He never carried it again. Here's an evening waistcoat, white on this side, black on the other. In a moment he could turn from a guest to a waiter. Here's a brace-and-bit, bottle of rock-oil, gimlet, wedges—just slivers of wood, but how useful they can be—safe-keys. Quite a collection of those. His special opera hat.

Lord Alfred takes the hat and turns it over.

LORD ALFRED: What's special about it?

BUNNY: Open it and you'll see. It was his idea to make a dark lantern out of an opera hat. You can't carry a dark lantern with evening dress, and Raffles nearly always worked in evening dress. He said it gave him a sense of moral superiority to any constable who ventured to stop him. Look inside. See the metal socket attached to the crown. He always carried a candle in his pocket and all he had to do was fix it—so.

LORD ALFRED: I would have liked to meet your Raffles on a dark night.

BUNNY: And look here. This is a very special walking stick. What do you think of that—?

LORD ALFRED: I imagined a burglar did more climbing than walking.

BUNNY: And how right you are. This helps you to climb.

Bunny unscrews the ferrule and shakes out of the cane a diminishing series of smaller canes, like a fishing-rod, which he joins together. He takes off the tray a double hook of steel and attaches it to the tip of the top joint. Then he attaches the hook to the top of the open door.

Imagine that's a balcony. And now for the finest of Manilla ropes. (*He takes a coil of rope from the tray*) Fine enough to tie up a parcel and strong enough to risk your life on. See the foot loops. He could wear this round his waist and nobody could tell. I've even seen him waltz in it.

LORD ALFRED: You fascinate me, Bunny. I have the glimmerings of an idea. A glorious idea. An idea that would have appealed to Raffles.

There is a double knock on the outer door. Bunny seizes the tablecloth and throws it over the chest. The opera hat lies forgotten on a chair. A second knock, louder this time. The cane remains hanging from the door.

BUNNY: Come in.

The head porter of Albany, Smith, in tophat and tailcoat enters from the hall: a very sturdy man with a sergeant-major's air of authority and a sergeant-major's moustache.

BUNNY: What is it, Smith?

SMITH: Well, sir, being new in this situation I want to do what's right.

BUNNY: I'm sure you do.

SMITH: And Betteridge before he went off to the war told me as how Mr. Raffles always wanted him to report anything what struck him as unusual, Betteridge being a sensitive sort of man with a nose for such.

BUNNY: You've seen something unusual?

SMITH: I said to myself, sir, Betteridge might think it unusual. You see there's an elderly man lingering around. He asked for you, sir, and me knowing you were with his lordship here, I told him you was out, but he hasn't gone away, sir. He walks up and down the Ropewalk from the back door to the front. You could almost say, sir, that he prowls.

LORD ALFRED: A fine choice of words. I can see you are as sensitive as Betteridge.

SMITH: Thank you, sir.

BUNNY: What does he look like?

SMITH: Not a gentleman, sir.

BUNNY: Couldn't you be a little more precise? Fat or lean? Tall or short?

SMITH: I wouldn't say he was either fat or lean—somewhere between the two.

BUNNY: His height then?

SMITH: If you said about the middle height, sir, you wouldn't be far wrong, give an inch or two either way. There was one thing I noticed—he has a grey beard much like His Royal Highness's.

LORD ALFRED: Perhaps it is the Prince. My friend has ties in the highest society.

SMITH: Oh no, sir. His Royal Highness would never wear such tweeds as this man wears. I've never seen the like before in Albany.

BUNNY: By God, Bosie, I believe it's Inspector Mackenzie. Has he a Scotch accent?

SMITH: He has some sort of accent, sir. I wouldn't like to define it.

BUNNY: Tell him—tell him you've received a telegram that I've gone for a week to Boulogne. No. Better say to Monte Carlo—otherwise he'll be slipping across on a cheap excursion.

A footstep in the hall and Smith turns. An elderly bearded figure in atrocious tweeds appears in the doorway.

(*With a touch of dismay in his voice*) It *is* Inspector Mackenzie.

SMITH: What are you up to, my man, coming in without so much as a knock?

DETECTIVE: The law doesna knock, porter. The law enters.

BUNNY: What do you want, Inspector?

DETECTIVE: Oh, just a wee word or two, but I mickle doubt if you'd want them spoken in public.

BUNNY: You can go, Smith. But when this gentleman leaves see that he really leaves.

SMITH: That I will, sir, but if you want him thrown out . . .

BUNNY: No, no, one doesn't throw a policeman out.

SMITH: There's many a gentleman in Albany would be glad to lend a hand. Mr. Digby on Staircase C spent a night in the cells last Boat Race Night.

BUNNY: Mr. Digby mustn't be disturbed on my account.

SMITH: Well, if you say so, sir. (*He looks with scorn at the detective*) The tweeds alone deserve it.

Smith goes out through the hall and we hear the closing of the front door.

DETECTIVE: He'll come to no good end if he hasna maer respect for the law. And now perhaps this gentleman too will be guid enough . . .

BUNNY: This gentleman, Inspector, is my friend Lord Alfred Douglas, son of the Marquess of Queensberry. You'll have heard of the Marquess. He's put up many a boxing match for the aid of police charities.

DETECTIVE: All the same, sir, I wouldna think you'd lak a lord to hear what I hae got to ask you.

BUNNY: You can't blackmail me, Inspector. Lord Alfred knows all about my past.

DETECTIVE: (*He takes stock of the room while he speaks*) That's mair than I can say, sir. You askit for four counts to be takken into consideration at your trial, but I'm thinkin' you left out ane or twa that you workit wi' Mr. Raffles.

BUNNY: You never proved anything against Mr. Raffles. You ought to have the decency to let the dead sleep in peace. Mr. Raffles died like a hero.

DETECTIVE: Oh, we ken weel how the dead are all heroes, sir. There'll be thousands of heroes before this war is over, and the wounded, why they be just pensioners in Chelsea—a mickle somethin' for a lost leg and a mickle somethin' for a lost arm an' maybe an extra saxpence a week for baccy. Weel, there be still questions I'd have askit your great hero, Mr. Raffles, if he were here now.

The detective moves around the room as he speaks. He sees the opera hat on the chair and picks it up, but Lord Alfred holds out his hand.

LORD ALFRED: My hat, Inspector. (*The detective surrenders it.*)

DETECTIVE: An' what was the name you gave, sir? Lord . . . ?

LORD ALFRED: I gave no name. My friend presented you to me. I am Lord Alfred Douglas.

DETECTIVE: Ah, I thocht that was the monicker.

The detective looks at the tablecloth covering the chest. He twitches a corner of it with his eyes on the two men. It is as if he were sniffing for the smell of fear. Still holding a corner of the cloth he looks up at the photograph of the cricket team.

A pity he didna stick to cricket—though it's not the equal to ma mind of the true sport o' kings. I'd have takken him on at golf mysel' an' thrashed him. (*He turns, still holding the cloth*) Your name's weel known to· me, my lord. The Oscar Wilde case. You seem to mak a strange choice of friends.

LORD ALFRED: You are being impertinent, Inspector.

DETECTIVE: Ah weel, Lord Alfred, I hae a likin' for straightforward crime. It's cleaner than muckin' aboot wi' boys.

LORD ALFRED: (*amused*) That too has been the sport of kings.

DETECTIVE: Your English kings. Oh, I ken ma history books.

LORD ALFRED: James the First was Scottish.

DETECTIVE: Aye, but his mither was reared in France.

(*He picks up the corner of the cloth again*) Ah weel, you an'
I, we'll argue aboot history anither time. (*He whips the cloth
off the chest.*)

The Raffles Relics, eh. This would put your grand hero into
prison if he wasna deid. A braw pity it was the Boers got at
him before me.

BUNNY: How would you have charged him, Inspector? If
they are Raffles relics they belong to Raffles. You can't accuse
a man of stealing his own belongings.

DETECTIVE: Housebreaking implements. It's an offence to
hae them on the premises. (*In his turn he begins to name
them*) Brace-and-bit, gimlet . . .

BUNNY: He was fond of carpentry. All the pictures you
see here—he made the frames himself.

DETECTIVE: Rock-oil. Ye ken what that's for.

BUNNY: Indeed I do. That was for oiling his bat. I'm afraid
you know little about cricket, Inspector.

DETECTIVE: A life preserver. Now how will ye explain
that?

BUNNY: Mr. Raffles liked his steaks tender. He used to beat
them with it. You can see the stains of gravy.

DETECTIVE: Gravy stains, eh? And this rod hangin' on the
door. Maybe ye'd lak me to show ye the way it works?

BUNNY: No need. I've been showing it already to Lord
Alfred. Mr. Raffles was always afraid of fire in Albany. The

safety precautions are hopelessly out of date, so he made his own. With this he could always get out on to the roof of Burlington Arcade and so into Bond Street. Of course there's a bit of Royal Academy roof to pass, but Raffles always said that the Academy would put out any fire.

DETECTIVE: An' I dessay ye've tried it yoursel'.

BUNNY: Oh, we used to have an occasional fire practice.

DETECTIVE: An' this revolver?

BUNNY: Any gunsmith will tell you it's never been fired. Perhaps a technical breach of the regulations, but Mr. Raffles was always fond of amateur theatricals. I remember once he played the part of you at Lady Melrose's. Do you carry a revolver, Inspector?

DETECTIVE: No, but I hae a pretty brace of handcuffs which I find unco' useful. Ye ken Lady Axminster? She's muckle worrited about her pearls.

BUNNY: You should know me better, Inspector. Even in my misguided youth before Mr. Raffles reformed me I would never have touched pearls. You can't recut or melt down pearls and they have to be worn to keep their lustre. Can you see me wearing Lady Axminster's pearls? I've never been a transvestite, Inspector.

DETECTIVE: I thocht maybe ye might have larned about such goings on with Mr. Wilde in Reading Gaol. Or from his lordship here.

LORD ALFRED: You seem to have a poor opinion of me, Inspector Mackenzie.

DETECTIVE: Ah keep ma thochts to masel'. (*To Bunny*) Ye wouldna mind, sir, you being as innocent as a new-born bairn, if I took a wee peek aroun' your apartment?

BUNNY: Known as chambers, Inspector, in Albany. Have you a search warrant?

DETECTIVE: I've not. I thocht ye being such a braw innocent chiel wouldna cause me all that trouble. I can easy telephone a magistrate.

BUNNY: No, go ahead, Inspector. My bedroom is through there. My bathroom opens out of it, but I suspect you know your geography. The kitchen is up the stairs outside, but you'll want to leave that to the last in case I sport my oak on you.

The detective moves towards the bedroom door.

LORD ALFRED: May I come with you? My favourite game as a child was Hunt the Slipper.

The detective disdains to reply and shuts the bedroom door behind him.

You were superb, Bunny. You must be very used to the police. Have you really got Lady Axminster's pearls?

BUNNY: Of course not.

LORD ALFRED: Just before your porter arrived I had a wonderful idea. Ever since poor Oscar's trial I've been puzzling how to revenge him on my odious father. Now here I am with a cracksman as a friend. I want you to burgle my father's house. He's mean as hell, but he always has a lot of ready cash in his safe for baccarat. He won't accept an IOU from his best friend, so of course he has to be prepared to pay up himself—though I've never known him lose.

BUNNY: I was never any good as a cracksman without Raffles.

LORD ALFRED: But you can't imagine the depth of my beastly father's stupidity. You remember he couldn't even spell Sodomite on the card he left at Oscar's club. I'll help you. It will be as easy as robbing a blind man.

BUNNY: No, Bosie, I've lost my nerve for the game—half my nerve was knowing that Raffles was with me. I've never told you about the only time he left me to case a joint alone.

LORD ALFRED: I love your professional phrases. Case a joint. So picturesque.

BUNNY: The house was in Surrey. One of those sham Tudor stockbrokers' houses. Raffles was playing for the Gentlemen in Manchester. I got into the hell of a jam, practically taken with my fingers on the safe, and then suddenly there was Raffles. Rain had stopped play and he'd caught an express to London. You don't understand, do you, all he risked for me?

LORD ALFRED: Quite a few years, I suppose.

BUNNY: He would never have thought of that. But suppose the rain had stopped he would have ceased to be a Gentleman.

LORD ALFRED: Why? I don't . . .

BUNNY: He would have lost his place on the team.

LORD ALFRED: So he would in prison surely?

BUNNY: But without the disgrace. The Gentlemen would have understood a thing like that. Prison is like an act of God. It can happen to any man.

LORD ALFRED: How interesting. Morality is one of those things I've never been able to keep up with. It changes more quickly than the shape of one's lapels. But, Bunny, can we talk of serious things? Next week my abominable father . . . he's always cropping up and the only thing I can do is to change the adjective . . . my moronic father has a house party. Men only. For baccarat. Of course there may be one or two female appendages. Some men seem unable to go away for a weekend without carrying a woman with them. So thoughtless and egotistical. We have to be polite to them.

VOICE: Would it be his country house or his town house you plan to rob, Lord Alfred?

A. J. Raffles enters from the bedroom. He is wearing the hideous tweeds, but the beard has gone except for one patch. The two others stare at him in astonishment.

BUNNY: A.J.?

Bunny runs to Raffles and puts his hands on his shoulders.

BUNNY: But you are alive?

RAFFLES: Very much alive, Bunny, and in great need of a Sullivan.

Bunny rushes to the desk and fetches a box of cigarettes.

The first I've had in eighteen months. You've always been inclined to dispose of me prematurely, Bunny. You remember when I drowned in the Mediterranean under the eyes of old Mackenzie? By the way, these tweeds are quite his style, aren't they? I spotted them in a second-hand clothes shop in Harwich when I landed this morning. So this is Lord Alfred Douglas (*offering his hand*). I've read a lot about you, sir, in the *Cape Times*.

BUNNY: But Raffles . . . Spion Kop . . . that will stained with your blood . . .

RAFFLES: Not my blood, Bunny. The poor devil beside me had his face blown off, so I took the opportunity to exchange papers before the Boers got to me. Some of the blood was his, though just in case I had used a lot of tomato sauce on the paper the night before. I didn't think that they'd check the genuineness of blood on a battlefield.

LORD ALFRED: And the Boers got you, Mr. Raffles?

RAFFLES: The Boers got me, Lord Alfred, but they were no cleverer than poor old Mackenzie. In fact I took a souvenir away with me. (*Raffles takes a gold watch from his waistcoat pocket*) General Botha's, inscribed by President Kruger himself. I had to leave the chain behind.

BUNNY: Oh A.J., A.J., I feel alive again. But why, why did you dress up as Mackenzie?

RAFFLES: It was the sight of these hideous tweeds that did it. Besides it's better for Raffles to stay legally dead.

BUNNY: One thing worried me. Old Mackenzie's sniffle. You forgot his sniffle.

RAFFLES: Bravo, Bunny. My accent was a bit uncertain too. I can manage real Devonshire, very fair Norfolk and three Yorkshire dialects, but Scots—I don't know the difference between Highlands and Lowlands. I tried to remember some Burns, but all that came to mind was "Scots wa hae wi Wallace bled, Welcome to your gory bed," and I've had enough of gory beds. And now, Lord Alfred, what is all this about avenging Mr. Wilde?

LORD ALFRED: How did you hear that?

RAFFLES: This little gadget here. (*He goes to the wall and indicates the mouth of a blower*) What do you suppose this is?

LORD ALFRED: A blower to the kitchen, I suppose.

RAFFLES: It served that purpose once, but I thought of diverting it to the bedroom with a little electrical device for increasing the sound. It pays sometimes to be an eavesdropper.

BUNNY: You never showed me that.

RAFFLES: My dear Bunny, there have been times when I have felt a little jealous, and this was one of those occasions. Finding you with Lord Alfred . . .

BUNNY: How could you suppose, A.J. . . . ?

RAFFLES: Your friend dead and Lord Alfred's friend in exile . . . I felt a little insecure, Bunny, in spite of that black band. But you should never wear a thing like that with evening dress. I'm not conventional but it shocks me. One must choose carefully what conventions to defy.

BUNNY: (*pulling the band off*) It's gone. Never to return.

RAFFLES: Oh, I don't expect to rise from the dead again. That would shock the Archbishop.

LORD ALFRED: You asked me, sir, about my detestable father's house. The baccarat will be at his country house. I hope now that he has you to help him, Bunny will agree to a little burgling.

RAFFLES: Ah, but will I help him, Lord Alfred? I've had time for reflection as well as Bunny. I was in a kind of prison too. Stone rocks instead of stone walls. And open to the sky. "That little tent of blue that prisoners call the sky." That's a remarkable poem of Wilde's you have beside your bed, Bunny. It was another sort of sky for me—a merciless glaring sky above the dried veld. I've had two passions in my life, Lord Alfred. Cricket and burglary. I have been pretty good at both, but I've begun to wonder whether it's really possible to keep practising them together. (*Pause*) I believe your father's house is in Hertfordshire, a county singularly without character.

LORD ALFRED: It is.

RAFFLES: I once spent a very sad weekend at Hemel Hempstead.

Raffles goes and looks at the photo on the wall. He touches his bat with tenderness.

Lying out there on Spion Kop I had a dream, Bunny. The old Raffles would be dead and someone, perhaps with the insignificant name of Jones, would land at Harwich. He knows a little about cricket—in Cape Town he had shown some promise. Perhaps he could find his way into a minor county eleven. Perhaps he might even turn professional—I imagine we are pretty short of ready cash, Bunny? Who knows? After a time Jones's talents might be spotted. A good slow bowler and no mean batsman. He might at last find himself a place with the Players and bowl that pseudo-Gentleman Grace for a duck first ball. That would make him forget the 400 not out you are too young to remember. Do you know—lying flat with my nose on the burnt grass of Spion Kop, I imagined I was smelling the turf at Lord's on a hot summer's day.

BUNNY: They'd recognize you at once, A.J.

RAFFLES: You didn't recognize me in Mackenzie's beard. That fraud W. G. Grace—would you recognise him *without* his beard? (*Pause*) Where does your father keep his cash, Lord Alfred?

LORD ALFRED: A safe in his bedroom. A very old-fashioned one. Behind the painting of a dog in a basket by Landseer. That's all he cares for—dogs and pugilists. Will you do it, sir?

RAFFLES: And what will you get out of it, Lord Alfred?

LORD ALFRED: A story to make Oscar laugh.

RAFFLES: I prefer to work with men who want money. They are more reliable.

LORD ALFRED: Give me any share you like. I'll send it to Oscar. He's in Paris, miserably poor.

RAFFLES: I much admire your friend. He was reckless in the pursuit of one passion. It's even more reckless to be divided between two, but how is one to decide? There is such poetry and drama in them both, though the poets I think have only celebrated cricket. Do you remember Francis Thompson:

"For the field is full of shades as I near the shadowy coast—"

I was near enough on Spion Kop—

"And a ghostly batsman plays to the bowling of a ghost,
And I look through my tears on a soundless clapping host
    As the runstealers flicker to and fro,
    To and fro,

O my Hornby and my Barlow long ago."

Thank God he didn't add Grace, but he should have seen *me* at my best, Bunny. And then there's Newbolt, a fine poet underrated by writers of your school, Lord Alfred.

> "There's a breathless hush in the Close tonight—
>   Ten to make and the match to win—
> A bumping pitch and a blinding light,
>   An hour to play and the last man in.
> And it's not for the sake of a ribboned coat,
>   Or the selfish hope of a season's fame,
> But his Captain's hand on his shoulder smote . . ."

I don't much like that last line. It smacks too much of Inspector Mackenzie. (*Pause*) I think I could be happy enough with cricket and to hell with burglary, Bunny, but what would you do all the long summer?

BUNNY: I'd be in the crowd cheering your hat trick or your century.

RAFFLES: You see, Lord Alfred, Bunny votes for cricket.

LORD ALFRED: There's not only my disreputable father's cash in the house, Mr. Raffles. There are always a few doxies around with their diamonds and their gold bracelets. Think what a fool he'd look if you *looted* the place.

RAFFLES: It's a good thing the summer's nearly over. I'll have a lot of work to do at the nets, Bunny, before I try my luck again. I've still got a bit of shrapnel in the left shoulder, but a spot of surgery will soon put that right.

BUNNY: Thanks to you I think I've got enough to see us through the winter.

RAFFLES: Ah, those winters, Lord Alfred. The winters Bunny and I have had together, here in old Albany. No women

to trouble our peace like Byron had. A wood fire. A Wisden to
set our memories working over a glass of old Madeira. Then a
leisurely dinner at the Café Royal round the corner, making
our last plans over a Château Lafite. And then a hansom to
the dangerous suburbs. You as a poet, Lord Alfred, will appre-
ciate that burglary has poetry as much as cricket. An unknown
house—all houses after midnight are unknown, however much
you've examined them in sunlight. Will there be a watch-dog
in the garden? No, not in suburbia. Here's a grass border. (*He
acts the whole affair*) Walk it as you'd walk a plank. Gravel
makes a noise and flower-beds tell a tale. Never use the heel.
(*He arrives at the door and the dangling cane*) Up there, look,
there's a balcony. This cane will prove useful. Or perhaps the
front door is an easy one to open with the right tool. Think of
the broad staircase that faces you, leading up from the dark
hall. No voices from the servants' quarters, a murmur from
the dining-room. Here they sit late and sleepy over the wine.
Give me my opera hat, Bunny. I must light a candle. These
shoes were specially made by Lobb's. They never give a tell-
tale squeak. I am on the first landing now. The room on the
left looks out on to the garden, but who sleeps in it? No day-
light inspection could tell that.

BUNNY: Where am I, A.J.?

RAFFLES: Where you ought to be, of course. Up on the
balcony with the rope fixed to the rail. There must always be
two ways of escape.

LORD ALFRED: Every guest will have brought cash to pay
his losses. No IOUs. There will be thousands of pounds in the
house that night.

RAFFLES: The cracksman is worthy of a poet, Lord Alfred.
The French have Villon, but there's a sad gap in our literature,
though I've sometimes thought that Francis Thompson had

Inspector Mackenzie and me in mind when he wrote *The Hound of Heaven*.

"I fled him down the nights and down the days,
I fled him down the arches of the years."

I'm not convinced of the existence of God, but I'm quite sure of Inspector Mackenzie.

"Still with unhurrying chase
And unperturbed pace"

—a fine description of a Scotland Yard flatfoot.

LORD ALFRED: The house party arrives on Friday.

RAFFLES: (*taking the ball out of the net and twisting it in his hands*) Burglary or cricket. What a choice! It's the same game, really. One man's skill against another's, and luck always taking a hand. "Ten to make and the match to win." Surely this is going to be the tired ball I've been waiting for. The moment's come to step out of the crease and smash it to the boundary—or is it not so simple as it looks? Is there a trap there? All the field's alert, but what's the good of a drawn match? I hate stonewalling. The risk makes the game. The risk, Lord Alfred. (*Pause*) I'll need a list of all the house guests and the rooms they occupy.

LORD ALFRED: I can get it from the housekeeper tomorrow.

RAFFLES: And a plan of the house floor by floor.

LORD ALFRED: I'll draw you one now if you'll give me a sheet of paper.

Lord Alfred sits down at the table. Bunny gives him a sheet of paper. Lord Alfred begins to draw.

RAFFLES: Are our bicycles in trim for a country ride, Bunny? It's not the job for a hansom.

BUNNY: They are.

RAFFLES: My Beeston Humber and your Royal Sunbeam, and the good Dunlop tyres. They leave tracks like a rattle-snake, Lord Alfred, but they are the most popular brand—nothing to distinguish our snake from all the other snakes on a wet road. (*Thoughtfully*) What a devilishly clever tempter you have always been. You tempted your friend Wilde to defy your father—the Scarlet Marquess they call him, don't they? —and Wilde ended in Reading Gaol.

LORD ALFRED: Are you afraid?

RAFFLES: Of course I'm afraid. Very much afraid. What poetry would be left in life if one couldn't feel fear?

LORD ALFRED: (*pointing at his plan*) This is my father's bedroom. Here's the Landseer painting I told you about. Behind is the safe. Very old. Easy to open.

SLOW CURTAIN

Act II

A bedroom in the Marquess of Queensberry's country house. A little light is coming through an open door in the right wall leading to a dressing-room and bathroom. Standing out from the back wall is a double bed. On the wall to the left of it hangs a Landseer painting, and to the right of the bed a door leads to the passage outside. A dressing-table stands beside the dressing-room door, and on the left of the room double curtains hide double windows and a balcony. The room is in darkness, except for the light from the dressing-room, and it is empty when the curtain rises. After a moment furtive sounds —scratches and rubbings and the clink of metal—come from behind the curtains.

They cease abruptly when there is a knock on the door. The door to the passage opens and a waiter, a young fair-haired man with a moustache, enters. He carries a bottle of champagne in an ice-bucket shoulder high. He turns on a centre light by the door, goes and looks through the door of the dressing-room and then puts the tray down on the dressing-table. A gold box on the dressing-table catches his eye. He lifts the lid and looks inside. At that moment a sneeze sounds behind the curtains. He hastily puts the box down and leaves, turning out the light. A short period of silence, and then the furtive noises begin again. The curtains sway, a voice says, "Damn!"

Bunny emerges in evening dress with a cloak. He has the

*end of a cord in one hand and an opera hat reversed in the
other—the Raffles relic—with a candle burning inside it. He
blows out the candle, drops the end of the rope and kicks it
out of sight behind the curtain. Then he inspects the room, as
the waiter did, peering first into the dressing-room. Next he
identifies the picture on the back wall and is about to lift it
down when he is disturbed by a knock on the door. He hastily
retreats behind the curtain. The door to the passage opens,
and this time it is Raffles in evening dress who enters and
turns on the light. He too carries a tray with a bottle of champagne on ice. Unlike the waiter he carries it unprofessionally
in both hands. He pauses at the dressing-table and is a little
disconcerted at the sight of the other bottle. He hesitates and
then puts down his ice-bucket beside the other. He sees the
gold box. He lifts it in his hands and mentally weighs it.*

BUNNY: *(entering from behind the curtains)* A.J.!

RAFFLES: Admirably on time, Bunny.

BUNNY: You've forgotten to turn your waistcoat and
where's your black tie?

RAFFLES: I saw myself in the glass and couldn't bear it. A
hero of Spion Kop can become a Chelsea pensioner, but never
a waiter. Anyway, I intend to mingle with the guests, Bunny.

BUNNY: Carrying a bottle of champagne on a tray?

RAFFLES: I admit I took that in a misguided moment. And
now there seems to be one bottle too many.

BUNNY: And one waiter too many. I thought it was you
for a moment.

RAFFLES: I'm sorry. One should never improvise. I followed a fellow to the cellar and I couldn't resist snatching a

bottle myself—there was a tray handy. I quite forgot I was a guest and not a waiter, but no harm's done. Now sketch me the battlefield, Bunny. The rope safely attached to the balcony?

BUNNY: Of course. There's a dressing-room through there and a bathroom beyond. And look, A.J., there's the Landseer.

RAFFLES: And here's a very handsome gold box. Not in the best of taste, but melted down . . . I bet you it weighs around a hundred ounces. And some diamonds of the first water in the lid. A plume and feathers. Obviously a present from the Prince of Wales. It sounds unpatriotic, but I long to pry them off, Bunny.

BUNNY: Are they large enough to recut?

RAFFLES: The best ones are. There's a smut on your nose, Bunny. That doesn't go with evening dress.

BUNNY: It was an infernal scramble to get on to the balcony. What first, A.J.? We'd better move fast.

RAFFLES: Bunny, Bunny, you've forgotten all my lessons. One must never burgle in a hurry. Bad for the nerves, like putting on your pads too soon. The men are all sitting down happily to their baccarat. The Scarlet Marquess never goes to bed before one.

BUNNY: But look at the dressing-table. Scent. Powder. All sorts of frippery.

RAFFLES: Either the Scarlet Marquess takes after his son or he's got a woman with him. That's awkward. You can never depend on a woman's bedtime. A sick headache, a quarrel with her lover. Life would really be so much easier without them.

While Raffles talks he has moved across the room and taken down the Landseer, disclosing a small safe. He leans the Landseer against the head of the bed.

A nice old-fashioned model. My safe-keys, Bunny. Burroughs of Birmingham. Went out of business in the fifties. Those dear old trustful times.

Raffles tries a few keys before finding the right one. He opens the door of the safe and gazes in with satisfaction.

How satisfying the sight of gold is. To think there are economists who want a paper currency. Bunny, that gold box on the dressing-table. Bring it here. Gold cries for gold.

BUNNY: It's full of letters.

RAFFLES: Get rid of them then. No, no, Bunny, not on the floor. In your pockets.

Raffles begins to fill the box with sovereigns.

BUNNY: Let's be off, A.J. The box alone . . .

RAFFLES: (*handing him the box*) There. Put that under your cloak.

Raffles begins to fill his pockets with coins. Bunny opens the door of a large wardrobe full of women's dresses.

BUNNY: A.J. For God's sake, look. This is a *woman's* room.

RAFFLES: I can hear a woman talking in the passage. That damned friend of yours! Quick, Bunny, on to the balcony.

Raffles closes the safe and turns out the centre light. He follows Bunny. The Landseer remains leaning against

*the head of the bed. The door opens and a lady in a
long sweeping evening gown stands silhouetted against
the light of the passage. She is around thirty years old
with great beauty and poise. She crosses to the dressing-table and looks at herself in the glass. An invisible
spot demands attention: some cotton wool from a
drawer, a squeeze with the fingers, a touch of alcohol
from a bottle, another examination, a dab of powder.
She sits down at the dressing-table and undoes her
elaborate coiffure. She puts a jewelled ornament she
has worn in her hair into a drawer. Her hair hangs down
to her waist. There is a tap on the door.*

LADY: Come in.

*A young lady's maid enters. We can soon tell from her
manner that she is devoted to her mistress.*

MAID: You never rang, ma'am.

LADY: I don't really need you tonight, Mary. You were up
very late yesterday.

MAID: I'm not a bit tired, ma'am. You'll never manage . . .

LADY: I undressed myself easily enough before I married. I don't suppose I've forgotten how.

MAID: You'll get yourself all tangled up. I'm sure you
will.

LADY: Well, go and turn on my bath and we'll see.

*The maid goes through the dressing-room door and we
hear a distant tap running. The lady gets out of her
dress easily enough. She goes and lays it on the bed.
She has an air of happiness and relaxation. She sings to*

*herself as she sits again at the dressing-table, undoes
her flowered garters, which she leaves under the looking glass. The song is a sentimental drawing-room ballad
which will be made famous later by Yvette Guilbert.*

(*Singing*)

"I will give you the keys of heaven,
I will give you the keys of heaven,
Madam, will you walk? Madam, will you talk?
Madam, will you walk and talk with me?"

*She pulls off her long stockings and plays with them
thoughtfully, swinging them in time with her song.*

"Though you give me the keys of heaven,
Though you give me the keys of heaven,
Yet I will not walk; no, I will not talk;
No, I will not walk or talk with thee."

*The lady drapes her stockings over the chair, but now
she has a little difficulty with her stays. She gets up and
looks for aid in a long pier glass, but after a short
struggle she loses interest for a moment in the stays as
she regards her own image and sings to it. The tap is
turned off.*

"I will give you a coach and six,
Six black horses as black as pitch."

*The maid comes to the door carrying a dressing-gown
of rose-coloured silk. She watches her mistress with
amusement.*

"Madam, will you walk? Madam, will you talk?
Madam, will you walk and talk with me?"

MAID: (*singing*)

"Though you give me a coach and six,
Six black horses as black as pitch;

Yet I will not walk; no, I will not talk;
No, I will not walk or talk with thee."

LADY: Why, what a pretty voice you have, Mary.

MAID: (*helping with the stays*) You see, ma'am, it's not so easy to undress yourself as you thought.

The curtain moves as Raffles makes a crack to see through. The maid as she folds up the stays notices the curtains move and goes towards the window.

Oh, ma'am, there's quite a cold draught from the window. I'd better close it.

LADY: (*as she gets out of her big drawers*) No, let it be, Mary. He likes the room fresh. He says it makes the bed warmer. Besides he likes to smoke his last cigar.

MAID: (*a little shocked*) A cigar? In the bedroom, ma'am? But do you like that?

LADY: (*a little sadly*) I like what he likes, Mary.

MAID: That's love, isn't it? Real love.

LADY: Yes, I suppose it is.

She is quite naked now. The maid approaches her, carrying the dressing-gown, but stops a moment before draping it over her to look at her mistress with admiration.

LADY: What is it, Mary?

MAID: (*singing softly*)

"I will give you the keys of my heart,
And we will be married till death us do part;
Madam, will you walk? Madam, will you talk?
Madam . . ."

Something in the song now has touched her mistress on the raw. She snatches the dressing-gown from the maid and speaks abruptly.

LADY: That's enough, Mary. Go to bed.

She moves to the dressing-room door but relents before she leaves and speaks kindly.

LADY: Good night. Sleep well.

MAID: (*a little dashed, the brief intimacy over*) Good night, ma'am.

She leaves the room. A few moments pass.

Raffles comes from behind the curtains followed by Bunny. They speak in low voices.

RAFFLES: You clear off by the balcony, Bunny. Where are the bicycles?

BUNNY: Hidden in the shrubbery to the left of the door as you come out. I'll be waiting for you there.

RAFFLES: No. You'll leave at once with that box.

BUNNY: I don't leave unless you come with me.

RAFFLES: Don't be an ass. How can I leave with all that lovely money lying around the baccarat table?

BUNNY: Somebody's sure to spot you, A.J. These are the sort of fellows who go to Lord's.

RAFFLES: Only bishops go to Lord's. Besides, I'm dead, Bunny, don't you realise that? I'm dead.

BUNNY: You've always said there must be two ways of escape. I'll guard the balcony until you are clear.

RAFFLES: It's not the young woman, is it, Bunny? Tell me the truth. I grant you she has the slender flanks of a young fawn.

BUNNY: What a fool you are, A.J.! Have I ever looked twice at a woman?

RAFFLES: Well, I thought that you looked rather more than twice from behind the curtain.

BUNNY: First you were jealous of Bosie, and now—this female object.

RAFFLES: I've been occasionally attracted by a female object myself. In the absence of a good chef, Bunny, they serve to warm the soup. (*Voice singing again*) She would have made a nice choirboy if she had cut off all that redundant hair.

A soft knock on the door to the passage.

Back, Bunny. (*Bunny hesitates*) Go on, you ass. No argument. I can manage this. (*A second knock*) Take the box and get back to Albany.

Bunny disappears behind the curtains. A rattle as he retrieves the rope. A third knock, louder this time.

VOICE: Alice, it's Bertie.

The door opens and a bearded figure, familiar to all the world, stands in the doorway.

RAFFLES: (*with an astonishment he can't conceal*) Your Royal Highness.

The somewhat stout figure of the Prince of Wales advances with ponderous authority into the room.

PRINCE: Who the hell are you? (*The Prince speaks with a heavy Teutonic accent.*)

RAFFLES: Jones.

PRINCE: Jones? What Jones?

RAFFLES: I know it's a somewhat *usual* name, Your Royal Highness.

PRINCE: My name is Portland, Mr. Portland.

RAFFLES: I thought . . .

PRINCE: I advise you not to think along those lines, Mr. Jones. I am Mr. Portland.

RAFFLES: (*obediently*) Mr. Portland.

PRINCE: And now what the hell are you doing in this room?

RAFFLES: I understood it was Lord Queensberry's room, sir. He asked for champagne.

PRINCE: It is Lord Queensberry's room. But he has been kind enough to lend his room to a friend of mine. (*He goes to the dressing-table and looks at the two bottles of champagne*)

Did Lord Queensberry order two bottles? That's most unlike him. (*The Prince examines one bottle*) Pommery. A very common Pommery.

RAFFLES: I felt sure there had been a mistake, Mr. Portland, so I brought another bottle. Mumm '84.

PRINCE: By God, you are an intelligent fellow, Jones.

The Prince goes to the dressing-room door and knocks. There's no reply—only the sound of splashing. The Prince knocks again.

PRINCE: Alice, how much longer are you going to be?

LADY'S VOICE: Only two minutes, Bertie.

PRINCE: Only two minutes! Multiply that by ten, Jones, and you'll be near the truth.

The Prince sits down by the dressing-table.

PRINCE: By the way, how is it that you are wearing a white tie? And a white waistcoat?

RAFFLES: I haven't got black ones, sir.

PRINCE: What sort of a waiter are you?

RAFFLES: An amateur one, sir. I'm sure you know what it is to be temporarily short of funds. I put my name down at an agency. Extra assistance was required here in a hurry, and I quite forgot about the tie—and the waistcoat.

PRINCE: You mean that's your own suit? You've got a good tailor, Jones.

RAFFLES: I'm afraid, sir, it smells of mothballs. I have been away in South Africa.

PRINCE: Looking for diamonds?

RAFFLES: Wounded and taken prisoner at Spion Kop, sir.

PRINCE: You were there? Why, sit down, my man, and tell me more. A soldier mustn't stand in front of a non-combatant.

RAFFLES: I would rather stand, sir, in your case.

PRINCE: Sit down, I said.

RAFFLES: If it's a command . . .

PRINCE: It is.

Raffles sits.

PRINCE: Your name is Jones, eh?

RAFFLES: As certainly, sir, as yours is Mr. Portland.

PRINCE: Ach! What regiment?

RAFFLES: Mounted Light Infantry, sir.

PRINCE: An amateur soldier as well as an amateur waiter. Your commander?

RAFFLES: Colonel Thorneycroft, sir. Under General Woodgate.

PRINCE: You were in the first assault then?

RAFFLES: Yes, sir. With some Lancashire companies and the Royal Engineers.

PRINCE: So you really were there, Jones. You mustn't mind my questions. I've met a good few beggars in Piccadilly who claim to have been at Spion Kop. Are you South African?

RAFFLES: No, sir. But I enlisted at Cape Town.

PRINCE: What were you doing there?

RAFFLES: To you, Mr. Portland, I would like to tell the truth. I was travelling abroad for my country's good.

PRINCE: Ach! I've done a bit of that myself. We seem to have more than one thing in common, Jones. (*The Prince takes out a cigar case*) Have a cigar. Alice is a good girl. She lets me smoke.

RAFFLES: If you don't mind, Mr. Portland, I'd rather have a Sullivan.

Raffles too takes out a case and the two men light up.

PRINCE: I think you and I might try the champagne.

RAFFLES: You honour me too much, sir.

PRINCE: I wish I could honour every man who fought at Spion Kop. I think for us, Jones, the Mumm. Pommery is good enough for the ladies.

Raffles opens the bottle and serves the wine.

PRINCE: How did you escape?

RAFFLES: It's not so hard, sir, from a Boer prison. I've been in tighter spots at home. I even brought away a souvenir. (*He takes out his watch and hands it to the Prince*) I had the honour of being interrogated by General Botha himself.

PRINCE: (*examining watch*) Louis Botha . . . President Kruger . . . By God, Jones, you're a man after my own heart. I only wish I could show this to my mother. It would make the old lady's eyes sparkle.

RAFFLES: Give it to her, Mr. Portland.

PRINCE: No, no . . .

RAFFLES: I would be proud to feel that I had given her a moment's pleasure.

PRINCE: Impossible. You earned this at Spion Kop.

RAFFLES: She has earned it, Mr. Portland, more than any of us.

PRINCE: You make me ashamed, Jones. If you ever need a reference . . .

RAFFLES: I'll write to Mr. Portland.

PRINCE: What address?

RAFFLES: London W. I think would be sufficient, sir.

PRINCE: Must I call it a present from Private Jones?

RAFFLES: Corporal Jones, sir. Say one of the *English* Joneses.

PRINCE: Do you know, if it wasn't for my mother, you and I wouldn't be talking together here. You see, I made her a rash promise a few years back to play no more baccarat. Presumably, Jones, you have been blessed with a mother?

RAFFLES: She died too early, sir, for me to have encountered her socially.

PRINCE: Ach! She talked to me very severely about gambling. I tried in vain to persuade her that a game of baccarat played by rich men for stakes they can afford is no more gambling than a bottle of champagne at dinner is alcoholism. Oh well, I've kept my promise. We've been playing bridge all the afternoon. Naturally the boys down there wanted to change to something stronger, so up I came to talk to Alice.

RAFFLES: I'm hardly such good company.

PRINCE: Well, one doesn't want to talk to a lady about Spion Kop. (*The Prince picks up the garters from the dressing-table, and lays them down again*) What an awful muddle, Jones, that was. Poor General Woodgate. I knew him slightly. He was lucky to die.

RAFFLES: I was lying close by when they came to carry him away, shot through the eye. I heard him sobbing, "Let me alone. Let me alone."

A long pause.

PRINCE: I have a German nephew, Jones. An intolerable ass. He fancies himself as a soldier and laughs at me as a useless non-combatant. This tummy of mine would have made a good mark, wouldn't it, on Spion Kop? The papers jeer at General Buller for his incompetence, but I doubt if Mr. Portland would have done any better—nor my nephew Willy either.

RAFFLES: I think I have seen photographs of your nephew, sir. A rather brazen moustache.

PRINCE: And probably sitting on a white horse. He had the effrontery once to write to my mother . . . why does one tell family secrets to Mr. Jones?

RAFFLES: Perhaps because I am like a stranger in the train. Once in everyone's life a man feels the need of a stranger in the train.

PRINCE: My strangers have generally been women. They are wonderful listeners. Do you know, my nephew had the effrontery to write to my mother that an honorary colonel of the Prussian Hussars had no right to be embroiled in a gambling case?

RAFFLES: Should I have been addressing you, sir, as *Colonel* Portland?

PRINCE: Ach! You know, Jones, these foreign uniforms they send me, they never fit. They call me Tum-Tum behind my back, but they never allow for it in their measurements.

He gets up and goes to the dressing-room door. He knocks again.

Alice! You've kept me long enough. (*Pause. He puts his ear to the door*) Two minutes still. She's got that boat in the bath with her. She calls it the *Britannia*. She likes sailing it up and down between her legs. Scylla and Charybdis she calls them. I've been wrecked there sometimes myself. (*He comes back and sits down*) Another ten minutes at least. Good women have such a passion to be clean. If they only knew what really takes our fancy. (*Again unconsciously he picks up the garters*) Do you know Paris well?

RAFFLES: I've spent a little time there.

PRINCE: Do you know La Goulue at the Moulin Rouge?

RAFFLES: I haven't had that chance, sir.

PRINCE: A fine, fine woman. I can talk to her as I can talk to you—as if I were real.

RAFFLES: Aren't we all real, sir?

PRINCE: I will tell you a parable, Jones. Once I took a walk with friends in the East End of London. I saw the very poor and how they lived. When I tried to give them money my friends hustled me into a cab. I was wrong, of course. You don't, if you think, give a starving cat milk, and you can't solve the problem of poverty with a handful of guineas. But what hurt me was that I had come there to talk to them, and my friends had carried me around like a wooden doll. I wasn't real any more than a plaster image in a Roman church. To be real for a little while we have to pretend . . . that you are Jones and I am Mr. Portland. I like women—because they let one pretend. It's only with a chance encounter like ours one can speak of Spion Kop and La Goulue in the same breath. The dying of poor Woodgate and the dancing of La Goulue. A dancer's honour and a soldier's honour. My father wouldn't have understood the connexion, and I'm quite sure my son doesn't. You and I, Jones, belong to a very special moment of time. *La Fin de Siècle* the papers call it, don't they? But it's more than just the end of any century. I have an awful fear that my nephew Willy, with his talk of Huns and Attila and inspiring fear, represents the future. I prefer my old mother . . . and senseless honourable Spion Kop. And La Goulue, of course. (*Pause*) You'd better go back to your job, Jones. I don't want you to lose it by keeping a lonely man company for . . .

A rush of feet along the passage outside and a furious beating on the door.

MAN'S VOICE: Sir, let me in. Let me in, sir.

PRINCE: The Scarlet Marquess. (*In a louder voice as the knocking is repeated*) The door is not locked, Queensberry.

The man who enters, the Marquess of Queensberry, is a small man with curly red hair, heavy eyebrows and long whiskers, and a heavy ugly lower lip. He is in a state of great excitement.

MARQUESS: Sir, there's an inspector from Scotland Yard downstairs.

PRINCE: Of course there is. I carry policemen about with me like an umbrella.

MARQUESS: This is not one of your troop, sir. There's a Special Branch man with him.

PRINCE: Just anarchists again, I suppose. Is it me or you they want to blow up?

MARQUESS: The inspector says there's a plot to rob your friend.

PRINCE: Alice, poor girl? I doubt if all her jewellery is worth a hundred pounds.

Throughout the conversation Raffles remains seated with his back to the Marquess and the door. The Marquess sees the Landseer propped up on the bed. He gives an anguished cry.

MARQUESS: My Landseer!

PRINCE: Your what?

MARQUESS: Who put it on the bed?

The Marquess runs to the safe taking a key from his pocket, opens it.

MARQUESS: I've been robbed.

PRINCE: So it was you not Alice they were after. I'm glad.

MARQUESS: But I've been robbed, sir.

PRINCE: So you have mentioned.

MARQUESS: Five hundred pounds gone.

PRINCE: Only bank cashiers calculate exact amounts of money without vulgarity. Just leave it that you've been robbed. Now have a glass of your excellent champagne.

MARQUESS: You sit there swilling my champagne as though nothing important had happened. Don't you understand, sir, what five hundred pounds means?

PRINCE: I begin to understand what it means to you.

The Marquess rushes into the passage and can be heard calling "Inspector, Inspector."

PRINCE: One must forgive him, Jones. The Marquess consorts too much with pugilists for his manners.

The real Inspector Mackenzie appears in the doorway with the Marquess behind him. The imitation by Raffles was not a bad one. His tweeds are as bad, but his accent is a lot less pronounced and is of course genuine Scots. He is much given to loud nose-blowing with a large bandanna handkerchief.

INSPECTOR: Inspector Mackenzie, Your Royal Highness.

PRINCE: (*not rising*) I am Mr. Portland in this house, Inspector. Please remember that.

MARQUESS: Look there, Inspector. My safe broken open. Five hundred pounds gone.

The Inspector approaches the safe in a heavy leisurely way. He blows his nose and looks inside.

INSPECTOR: Not *broken* open, my lord. There are a few sovereigns left. Five, six, a round dozen maybe. The thief seems to have been disturbed.

MARQUESS: Aren't you going to take fingerprints?

INSPECTOR: Oh, every thief kens all aboot fingerprints, sir. That Monsieur Bertillon taught 'em to wear gloves. I niver fash mysel' to carry pouder around with me.

Raffles remains seated near the Prince with his legs crossed and his back turned to the Inspector.

INSPECTOR: How long would you hae bin here, Your . . . sir?

PRINCE: Ten minutes. Perhaps a quarter of an hour.

The Inspector goes and draws back the curtains. Raffles watches him over his shoulder. The windows are open.

INSPECTOR: We are on the first floor. It's not a long leap from the balcony. (*He moves forward through the window on to the balcony and a moment later returns trailing a rope with him)* He didna' need to leap. This is the way he came an' went. He's left his rope behind. A verra fine Manilla rope—it puts me in mind of a cracksman called Raffles who led me many a dance, but he's deid, God rest his soul, though I'd like to have takken him mysel' before God did.

PRINCE: You spoke of a plot, Inspector?

INSPECTOR: Yes, sir, I talked in London with a gentleman from the Special Branch. They deal with plots. I only deal with crime.

PRINCE: What sort of a plot?

INSPECTOR: Weel, it seems, sir, they hae an agent in the German Embassy. What we call an informer, an' he's told 'em that they are out to get certain letters.

PRINCE: Have you been indiscreet again, Queensberry?

MARQUESS: Indiscreet? When have I ever been indiscreet? God damn it, Inspector, five hundred pounds gone and you babble about letters.

INSPECTOR: It's not exactly your lordship who's concerned . . .

PRINCE: Well, who is? Come to the point, man.

MARQUESS: What's it all got to do with my safe? I didn't keep any letters there.

INSPECTOR: No, your lordship. These letters, well, it's like this, if the information is correct an' I'm not saying it is . . .

PRINCE: *(impatiently)* Inspector!

INSPECTOR: These letters were addressed to a lady staying here. A lady his lordship lent his room to.

PRINCE: What in heaven's name would the Germans want Alice's letters for?

INSPECTOR: To publish them in the German Press, sir. Mind you, that's what the Special Branch say.

PRINCE: (*with a loud laugh*) By God, it's possible. A typical idea of Willy's. I suppose I *would* look a bit foolish. One shouldn't write letters like that in prose, but we are not all poets like your son, Queensberry. All the same it hardly seems worth a plot. Poor mother, it's a pity she reads the German Press. My wife will only laugh. You know, Jones, or perhaps you don't, the laughter of someone you love can be a lot more painful than anger.

MARQUESS: I don't know what you are all talking about. He's stolen *five hundred pounds.*

PRINCE: If you must talk like a bank cashier, Queensberry, be accurate. Five hundred minus twelve.

INSPECTOR: Where were the letters kept, sir, if not in the safe?

PRINCE: The lady kept them, I believe, in a gold cigar box I had given her. It was a present to me from some friends in the theatre. It was decorated with my arms in diamonds, but as no doubt you know, Inspector, sandalwood is a much better receptacle for cigars than gold and diamonds. It was her whim to put my letters in the box instead of throwing them into the wastepaper basket as I advised her to do. They were really not worthy of so important a setting.

INSPECTOR: They were dangerous, sir?

PRINCE: They were worse, Inspector. They were badly written.

INSPECTOR: And this gold box, sir? She didn't keep it in that safe there?

PRINCE: No, no, the safe belongs to Lord Queensberry. We are only weekend guests.

INSPECTOR: Then where would she keep it, sir?

PRINCE: Well, the last time I saw the box—it was earlier this evening before dinner—I had come to take her down—I teased her a little about it.

INSPECTOR: Where was it, sir?

PRINCE: Here on the dressing-table.

INSPECTOR: And it's not there now.

PRINCE: No—now you mention it—it isn't.

INSPECTOR: Where is the lady, sir? With your permission I would like to ask her a few questions.

PRINCE: It would be a little inconvenient, Inspector. She is in her bath, or rather Lord Queensberry's bath—the only one in the house. If you don't mind waiting, I don't think she will be more than half an hour. She told me she would be two minutes a quarter of an hour ago.

INSPECTOR: (*looking at his notebook*) I think, sir, you said that you and this gentleman came up about that time.

PRINCE: Oh no. Mr. Jones was here when I arrived . . .

INSPECTOR: Here?

Raffles uncrosses his legs. He looks as if he might be preparing to rise.

PRINCE: He had brought me a rather better champagne than Lord Queensberry's first waiter had sent up. A very good Mumm '84.

MARQUESS: A Mumm '84! I've only two dozen bottles left. I provided no champagne. Neither you nor the lady asked for it.

PRINCE: Yet here are the two bottles. Perhaps your butler was more thoughtful than you.

MARQUESS: My butler does nothing without my orders. Who is this Mr. Jones?

Raffles makes to rise, but the Prince signals him to remain seated.

PRINCE: A gentleman I'm proud to have met who fought at Spion Kop.

MARQUESS: Where's Spion Kop?

PRINCE: I forgot, Queensberry, that while England has been fighting the Boers, you have been fully engaged fighting Mr. Oscar Wilde.

MARQUESS: I insist on knowing who this man is. This is my house.

RAFFLES: (*speaking over his shoulder without rising*) I am the second waiter with the Mumm '84, Lord Queensberry.

MARQUESS: How dare you sit there in my room like a gentleman?

RAFFLES: Mr. Portland ordered me to sit. Mr. Portland unlike you has a natural authority. So I sat and he hasn't asked me to rise.

MARQUESS: Who the hell are you? You aren't one of my men.

RAFFLES: Thank God, no.

The Inspector begins to approach.

RAFFLES: Forgive me, Mr. Portland, if I get up.

Raffles jumps to his feet and makes a dash for the window, but the Inspector is too quick for him. He takes him by the left shoulder and spins him round.

INSPECTOR: A. J. Raffles! Come back from the deid. It's lak an answer to prayer. Many a time I've prayed to the guid God to let me put my hands on you.

RAFFLES: Be careful of my shoulder, Mackenzie. There's still a bit of Boer shrapnel lodged there.

PRINCE: *Raffles*, Mr. Jones?

RAFFLES: I did hint to you, sir, that I was incognito like yourself.

PRINCE: *The* Raffles?

The Inspector as the Prince speaks has clapped on a pair of handcuffs.

RAFFLES: (*looking glumly at the handcuffs*) I haven't met another. I was an only child, but distant cousins of course are always apt to pop up.

PRINCE: I saw you in '96. At Lord's. 105 not out against Australia. You won us the Ashes.

RAFFLES: Well, I regret to say, sir, W. G. Grace also played a small but grandiloquent part.

MARQUESS: You infernal scoundrel, where is my money?

RAFFLES: I gather there are some twelve pounds still in the safe. As for the rest you can find some of them if you search me, but I would prefer the cleaner hands of Inspector Mackenzie.

The Marquess raises his hand to strike him.

PRINCE: (*sharply*) Marquess! Remember the Queensberry rules. You were really at Spion Kop, Raffles?

RAFFLES: Yes, sir, to you I have told no lies.

PRINCE: Take off the handcuffs, Inspector. This man has fought for his country, which is more than you or I have done.

MARQUESS: He's a common thief.

PRINCE: An uncommon one, I should say.

MARQUESS: He's robbed me and he's robbed you.

PRINCE: On the contrary he has given me a present of inestimable value. He will go quietly to Scotland Yard. I make myself responsible.

INSPECTOR: I'm afraid I can't obey you, sir.

PRINCE: You can't obey me?

INSPECTOR: I can't obey Mr. Portland, sir.

PRINCE: I shall not always be Mr. Portland.

INSPECTOR: I ken that weel, sir.

MARQUESS: Bravo, Inspector, no man is above the law, eh?

INSPECTOR: Verra true, my lord, but it doesna need all that emphasis.

RAFFLES: You know, I'm quite happy with these bracelets. A better lock than you had on your safe, Marquess. (*To the Prince*) I am sorry, sir, for disorganising your evening. It wasn't my intention. And if I had known that the gold box belonged to a friend of Mr. Portland . . .

MARQUESS: I hope you'll lock him up in your coldest cell for the night, Inspector.

INSPECTOR: We have our Queensberry rules too, your lordship. We charge him, he telephones—if that's what he wants—to his lawyer, an' then we give him a nice cup o' tea—and a sandwich if he feels so inclined.

RAFFLES: Oh, that won't be necessary, Inspector. I dined well at the Café Royal before I came. Your sandwiches, I fear, would be of the railway station variety.

MARQUESS: I'll get my coachman out of bed and drive you to London myself. I intend to see justice done on this scoundrel.

RAFFLES: (*to the Prince*) I think, sir, you are more interested in the letters than in the gold box?

PRINCE: One can buy a new box at Asprey's. I would hate to rewrite my letters.

RAFFLES: I think I might be able to recover the letters, sir.

MARQUESS: And my gold?

RAFFLES: Ah, that is a separate matter. Mr. Portland's interests must come first. There seems to be a basis for a bargain.

INSPECTOR: Ye canna bargain with the law, man.

RAFFLES: I'm told the Special Branch are sometimes more amenable. If I helped you to lay your hands on the mystery man . . .

INSPECTOR: The man with the rope?

RAFFLES: No, no, the waiter with the Pommery, of course.

A key turns in the dressing-room door and the lady enters singing softly with a towel wrapped round her waist. The song dies on her lips as she looks at the four men in the room.

LADY: Bertie, what on earth are all these people doing in *our* room?

CURTAIN

Act III

The chambers in Albany early next morning. Half dark. A light burning on the table. Lord Alfred Douglas asleep in an armchair. A key grates in the hall lock. Bunny enters, his evening dress in a very tousled condition.

BUNNY: Bosie!

Lord Alfred wakes with a start.

LORD ALFRED: My dear Bunny! You gave me quite a start, slinking in like a thief.

BUNNY: (*bitterly*) I am a thief.

LORD ALFRED: Oh yes, I had forgotten. It would have been more tactful to say "calling early like the milkman."

BUNNY: Raffles is caught.

LORD ALFRED: That's unfortunate.

BUNNY: It won't be long before the police are here. They know we always worked together.

Bunny opens the chest and returns the opera hat to the secret drawer.

I left the rope behind. I hoped Raffles would use it. I hid in the shrubbery with the bicycles, until I saw him driven away in handcuffs with Inspector Mackenzie and another man.

LORD ALFRED: The burglary failed?

BUNNY: Oh, we did what you wanted. While I was hiding I could hear your father baying like a pack of foxhounds for his money. Here it is. (*He takes the gold box from under his evening cloak*) Or part of it. By this time Inspector Mackenzie has the rest.

LORD ALFRED: Whose box is it?

BUNNY: Your father's, I suppose. A present from the Prince of Wales.

LORD ALFRED: Impossible. My father would have pawned it long ago.

BUNNY: Open it. You'll find about half the money he had in the safe.

LORD ALFRED: (*opening the box*) He'll be fighting mad.

BUNNY: Take your share and get out before the police come.

LORD ALFRED: No, I owe you an alibi. Put on your pyjamas and lend me a pair. We both spent the night here.

BUNNY: And go to prison like Wilde? I prefer felony. They treat felony better. I suppose everyone, even a judge, has stolen something in his time, if only a woman, but sodomy is beyond his imagination.

LORD ALFRED: The boat train from Victoria leaves at nine. Come with me, Bunny. Oscar's in Paris at the Hotel d'Alsace. He'll be glad to see us. Poor devil, he badly needs the money.

BUNNY: Take it all and clear out. I won't need it in jail, and at least they won't have *that* evidence. You've done enough harm, Bosie. Your errors of judgement always lead others to prison.

LORD ALFRED: What do you mean, Bunny?

BUNNY: There was a woman sleeping in your father's room.

LORD ALFRED: I suppose he keeps a whore. He's never been able to keep a wife.

BUNNY: This was no whore.

LORD ALFRED: How very odd. If you'd found a boxer, I could have understood it. My father has a passion for boxers —not in the interesting sense of the word. Revolting types with muscles like a coil of snakes and breasts like fat women at fairs. A broken nose or a cauliflower ear are marks of beauty to my disgusting parent.

BUNNY: There wasn't one woman on the guest list you gave us.

LORD ALFRED: Strange. A woman incognito. It wasn't our dear old Queen by any chance, was it?

BUNNY: It wasn't. I saw her undress.

LORD ALFRED: You seem to have had a *mouvementé* evening.

BUNNY: You find it amusing, don't you? Poor Raffles. He told me to take this box and go. He was so sure he could manage things. He always did manage somehow in the old days.

LORD ALFRED: I suppose even a burglar gets out of practice.

BUNNY: Be off, Bosie. It's not going to be so funny when the police arrive.

LORD ALFRED: But I've done nothing, Bunny. I've been innocently asleep. I had a dream of an enormous pineapple.

BUNNY: They'll make you out an accomplice before the fact or after the fact or both.

LORD ALFRED: My avaricious father stopped my allowance when I refused to leave Oscar. So you might say that this is part of his debt to me. I know man doesn't live by bread alone, but I've even had to give up caviare. Really, they can't charge me with drawing my own allowance. Anyway I don't much fancy Paris in a cheap hotel all alone with poor Oscar. Not necessarily alone either, though I shudder to think of what he can buy on two pounds ten a week. That's what his wife allows him.

BUNNY: All the more reason to take this and go.

LORD ALFRED: But what about Raffles' share?

BUNNY: The box will be our share, if I can hide it. It's worth more than the cash, but you wouldn't know the right market.

LORD ALFRED: I suppose it would save a bit of argument with the police if neither I nor the gold were here. I hate arguing with inferiors. They are so apt to raise their voices.

He begins to gather the money into his pockets.

BUNNY: Have a good time in Paris.

LORD ALFRED: I doubt if I shall. Oscar writes that the place is full of Americans and Germans. Do change your mind, Bunny, and come too.

BUNNY: I was alone for two years in prison without Raffles. I'm not going to let him suffer the same way.

Sound of the hall door closing. Footsteps in the hall. Bunny turns.

BUNNY: Too late, Bosie. Here they come.

The door opens, but it is not the police but the first waiter with the blond moustache who enters, still in his waiter's tails, wearing a black overcoat. When he speaks it is with a slight foreign accent.

WAITER: Excuse me. The door was open.

BUNNY: What are you doing here?

WAITER: I will explain, sir. You and I belong to similar services. I was hiding in the same bushes. There were two bicycles. You took one, I took the other.

BUNNY: You took Raffles' bicycle—his Beeston Humber? You're a damned thief.

WAITER: Those are not terms we employ in my service or yours.

BUNNY: What the hell are you talking about?

LORD ALFRED: I think I've met you somewhere before.

WAITER: Yes, my lord, that is true. At the Narcissus Club in Archer Street.

LORD ALFRED: Are you a waiter there?

WAITER: *Nein, nein.* I am a member like you, Lord Alfred. On a secret mission one suffers loneliness. No one to speak to. That is bad for the health. It is a security risk. So I go to the Narcissus Club, Archer Street. That was the address recommended by my service for agreeable uninquisitive company.

BUNNY: Would it be against security to tell me who you are?

WAITER: Between our services there is no question of security. (*He clicks his heels together*) Captain von Blixen of the Prussian Hussars. Seconded for a secret mission in England because of my knowledge of English. You, I believe, are Captain Yevgeny Petrovitch.

BUNNY: No.

VON BLIXEN: *Nein?*

BUNNY: *Nein.*

VON BLIXEN: In Berlin we are taught not to have secrets from fellow officers engaged on similar missions. Let the best man win as in chess.

BUNNY: It was you I saw between the curtains bringing the bottle of champagne.

VON BLIXEN: Yes, I did it well? Tray on the level of the right shoulder. I received special instruction at the Hotel Adlon. High commendation from the head waiter.

BUNNY: What on earth do you want? I warn you the police will be here any moment.

VON BLIXEN: Do not worry, Captain Petrovitch. We have much time to arrange our affair. I have studied very hard the methods of the English police. I took that course under a most distinguished professor, Dr. Heinrich Engelbeim, author of the classic work, *English Methods of Law Enforcement from Ethelred the Unready to Sir Robert Peel*. I was head of my class as at the Adlon Hotel. I have the impression, Captain Petrovitch, that they do not train so well at St. Petersburg. Your colleague was wearing a white tie, and he carried the champagne with both hands. And you—you sneezed behind the curtain. They did not teach you not to sneeze at St. Petersburg? *Nein?*

BUNNY: *Nein.*

VON BLIXEN: You disturbed me when you sneezed, Captain. Ah, I said at once to myself, that is Captain Yevgeny Petrovitch. Now we in Berlin are trained not to sneeze.

BUNNY: Bosie, is this fellow mad or am I mad?

LORD ALFRED: Tell me, Captain von Blixen, how do they train you not to sneeze? A finger on the upper lip?

VON BLIXEN: That is not to be relied on. It is not scientific. If you feel a sneeze about to arrive, you take a pin prepared by our great pharmaceutical firm of Bayer and you prick the nose. Close to the nostril. You see, (*he turns up his lapel*) here I carry pins. Three pins. It is the allowance for one mission.

LORD ALFRED: Suppose a fourth sneeze arrives?

VON BLIXEN: That would mean a real cold. We have a very strict examination before a mission and many injections.

LORD ALFRED: One catches cold very easily in England, Captain, even in summer.

VON BLIXEN: If I catch a cold, then I retire. Another takes my place.

LORD ALFRED: Trained at the Adlon?

VON BLIXEN: *Ja, ja.* Naturally.

LORD ALFRED: I once passed a happy weekend at the Adlon with Oscar. We little knew that the waiter who brought us our morning coffee might be training as an agent. It's true he proved very well trained in other ways. Please tell me, Captain von Blixen, what exactly are you after?

VON BLIXEN: That gold box on the table, Lord Alfred.

LORD ALFRED: And I suppose you think I am in competition with you? As a graduate of the St. Petersburg school.

VON BLIXEN: Not you, Lord Alfred. We know your interests very well. In Germany we are not hypocrites. We have much sympathy for you and much admiration for your great poet, Mr. Oscar Wilde. But this gentleman . . . that is a different affair. I can recognise the kind of inferior training he has received.

LORD ALFRED: At St. Petersburg?

VON BLIXEN: *Ja.* St. Petersburg.

BUNNY: Bosie, the man's mad.

VON BLIXEN: You and I, Captain Petrovitch, know that to pretend madness is part of the training of any agent. We understand each other—but the stupid police, they will think we are both mad. So we save the secret of our services. That I learnt in the psychology course under Professor Himmelstuber. I make myself clear? *Nein?*

BUNNY: *Nein.*

VON BLIXEN: And now the police will have finished their interrogation of your comrade. They will have broken him, or he will have taken his pill of cyanide. It is time for me and you to leave. So the gold box, please. (*He picks it off the table and opens it*) *Gott in Himmel,* it is empty!

LORD ALFRED: The money has been transferred to my pocket, Captain.

VON BLIXEN: Money? What money? I am not sent to steal money. Where are the letters?

LORD ALFRED: What letters?

VON BLIXEN: The letters were in the box. I saw them.

He draws a revolver from his pocket and points it at Bunny.

LORD ALFRED: Have you any letters, Bunny?

BUNNY: Why, yes, I suppose I have. (*He feels in his pockets*) Unless they've fallen out on the road. I remember a bump in Boxmoor High Street.

VON BLIXEN: You've dropped the letters? Then you are a disgrace even to St. Petersburg.

BUNNY: It comes of riding a bicycle in tails. They kept on getting caught in the brakes. There seem to be a few left.

VON BLIXEN: Give them to me.

BUNNY: Why should I?

VON BLIXEN: (*waving the revolver*) This is your excuse, Captain Petrovitch. An agent must never kill another agent, but I am permitted to shoot you in both legs.

BUNNY: You really do want the letters. Why? Who wrote them?

VON BLIXEN: Why pretend ignorance with me? That is not football.

BUNNY: Cricket.

Bunny begins to remove letters from his various pockets. Von Blixen snatches two of them and begins to read.

"My dear Alice. It was a bitter disappointment to me not to find you at Lady Melrose's party . . ." "Dearest of all Alices" —that is better—"Alas! I have an appointment with my tailor at three. That ass Willy has sent me another of his damned foreign uniforms . . ." (*Von Blixen's voice falls away with disappointment and embarrassment.*)

LORD ALFRED: Hardly worth a hold-up surely? Wouldn't you rather take the gold box?

VON BLIXEN: Do you think a captain of the Prussian Hussars can be bought with gold?

The Prince of Wales enters from the hall.

PRINCE: Put down that gun, Captain.

Von Blixen turns so that his gun points at the Prince.

VON BLIXEN: Your Royal Highness.

PRINCE: Your colonel, Captain. If only an honorary one. Please point your revolver in another direction. The ceiling is more suitable. Or the floor. (*Von Blixen drops his revolver on the table*) Thank you. I don't think the Emperor would have been pleased if you had shot his uncle. It would have been difficult to hush up—even in Albany. Lord Alfred, what is your part in all this?

LORD ALFRED: It's all my obnoxious father's fault, sir. I'm running out of adjectives. It's like rhymes for love.

PRINCE: What's your father got to do with it?

LORD ALFRED: He stopped my allowance, sir. So Mr. Raffles and my friend Bunny here—whom this gentleman insists on calling Captain Yevgeny Petrovitch—were good enough to offer their services and extract it for me.

PRINCE: And the letters?

BUNNY: We had nothing to do with the letters, sir. Only Captain von Blixen was interested in the letters.

PRINCE: They don't read aloud well, Captain. I'm glad you didn't reach the more passionate parts. I don't fancy seeing them published in the *Frankfurter Zeitung*.

VON BLIXEN: I have failed my Emperor. I shall resign my commission. I shall go to Africa.

PRINCE: If you are looking for lions, my dear fellow, you have only to go as far as Trafalgar Square.

von Blixen: Mock me if you must, Your Royal Highness, but beware that man (*pointing at Bunny*). Whatever he says, he is an agent of the Emperor Nicholas and his pockets are stuffed with your letters.

Bunny: I'm sorry. I don't think I have any more. Most of them fell out in Boxmoor High Street.

Lord Alfred: What has happened to Raffles, sir?

Prince: As far as I know he is on the roof with your father and Inspector Mackenzie.

Lord Alfred: Why the roof, sir?

An enormous crash of broken glass.

Prince: Ach! I hope they are not fighting among themselves. Raffles was convinced we should find this fellow here looking for my letters. He persuaded the Inspector to release him on parole and help block the escape route.

Bunny: Over the roof of the Burlington Arcade. A rather private way in an emergency. I doubt if the Captain knows of it.

Prince: (*to Lord Alfred*) It was not the Captain your father was concerned about. He was afraid your friend would escape with the box and the money. He insisted on accompanying Mr. Raffles and the Inspector. I came the conventional way helped by your friendly porter whom I found sleeping with an empty bottle of Spanish wine. I had to persuade him that I was not Inspector Mackenzie. He seemed to find a resemblance. Surely it can only be the beard? I haven't picked up a Scotch accent at Balmoral? No, no, Captain, please do not move. I want you to tell me why my nephew Nicholas would want my letters. Willy I can understand, but not Nicky.

VON BLIXEN: Everything my Emperor wants, Your Royal Highness, Russia always tries to snatch. One day it will be a war of armies—now it is a war of agents. This man has all the faults of the St. Petersburg school.

LORD ALFRED: The Berlin school has hardly done better . . .

Raffles enters through the bedroom door.

LORD ALFRED: What's happened, Raffles?

RAFFLES: Your father has fallen through the roof into the Burlington Arcade.

LORD ALFRED: (*hopefully*) Is he dead?

RAFFLES: I think so. I can't be sure. I thought I saw his leg twitch. Inspector Mackenzie is climbing down to see.

LORD ALFRED: Perhaps if I went to help I might be able to give him the *coup de grâce.*

RAFFLES: Unwise in the presence of the Inspector. So, as I told you, sir, you've found the waiter with the inferior Pommery. Have you recovered the letters?

PRINCE: Your friend seems to have dropped most of them in a place called Boxmoor.

RAFFLES: That's unfortunate. The waiter might return and recover them. That has to be prevented. Is that your revolver, waiter?

VON BLIXEN: I am not a waiter. I am Captain von Blixen of the Prussian Hussars seconded for special services.

RAFFLES: Allow me to borrow your revolver, Captain. (*He helps himself*) And now it will be my painful duty to ensure that you don't return to Boxmoor.

VON BLIXEN: It is no good to threaten me. Even death would be less hard than the thought that I have failed my Emperor.

RAFFLES: An admirable sentiment. I can hear Irving pronouncing it at the Lyceum. One thing, though, troubles me. Killing you is child's play, but how . . . how . . . do we dispose of your corpse?

LORD ALFRED: You could incinerate him.

RAFFLES: But I have no incinerator.

PRINCE: I have read that a bath of acid has sometimes been used, Mr. Raffles.

RAFFLES: In Albany? We shan't even have constant hot water for another twenty years.

BUNNY: I suppose we might dismember him. A head, two arms, two legs and a torso—they would fit into that chest.

RAFFLES: If only one of us were a surgeon. A job like that has to be done neatly. Otherwise all sorts of undesirable bits and pieces fall out.

Captain von Blixen is more and more uneasy.

LORD ALFRED: Surely, Captain Petrovitch, they taught you to carve at the St. Petersburg school?

RAFFLES: Petrovitch?

LORD ALFRED: It seems that this is Captain Yevgeny Petrovitch of the Russian Secret Police.

BUNNY: At St. Petersburg we only had bears to practise on. Perhaps I could manage if Captain von Blixen would look a little more like a bear. Another thing—we had proper surgical knives. Here I've only got a blunt bread knife. And a serrated edge may prove messy.

VON BLIXEN: I insist on being shot as an officer and a gentleman.

RAFFLES: Of course, of course, we are not barbarians. We will shoot you first, Captain. I wouldn't dream of letting him carve you up alive. But I'm troubled about the bloodstains you'll leave on the carpet.

PRINCE: Surely your friend could spread some newspapers on the floor. *The Times* is better for that than the *Telegraph*.

LORD ALFRED: I'm sorry, sir, the sight of blood always makes me feel ill. Besides, the Captain and I belong to the same club. With your permission, I will go and see if my infernal father is still alive. I might seize an opportunity of strangling him if the Inspector turns his back.

BUNNY: Better leave by the door, Bosie. You have no head for heights.

LORD ALFRED: If you will excuse me, sir. (*He leaves.*)

PRINCE: Strangling. Ach! That is quite an idea. It would avoid blood.

VON BLIXEN: I appeal to you, Your Royal Highness. As my honorary colonel. Grant me a clean death like a soldier.

RAFFLES: A *cliché*, Captain. A soldier's death is very seldom clean. By the way, is that your own suit? It doesn't fit you very well.

VON BLIXEN: It is a hired suit from the Brothers Moss in Covent Garden. If I have to die, please see that the suit is returned. They trusted me without a deposit.

RAFFLES: I don't like the idea of strangling, sir. All very well for Lord Queensberry—not for a man who dies in the service of your nephew.

PRINCE: I was merely making a suggestion. I don't insist, Mr. Raffles.

RAFFLES: I would feel like a hangman. Don't you agree, Captain Petrovitch?

BUNNY: Oh, in Russia a hangman's is an honourable profession.

RAFFLES: All the same, as between one agent and another, wouldn't it be possible to accept his word of honour—as a captain of the Prussian Hussars—that he will not bicycle back to Boxmoor?

VON BLIXEN: I will never give it. I would rather be cut up.

RAFFLES: Yevgeny Petrovitch.

Bunny comes to Raffles' side and Raffles whispers in his ear. Bunny goes to the bedroom and a little later comes back with several copies of The Times.

Your request is granted, Captain von Blixen. You will die a soldier's death and your clothes will be returned untarnished to Moss Bros. Take off your coat and your jacket. (*Von Blixen obeys*) Now would you remove what our great writer Mr. Henry James has called "the nether integuments of a gentleman"?

VON BLIXEN: I do not understand.

RAFFLES: Your trousers.

VON BLIXEN: *Nein, nein.* I refuse. If you shoot me through the heart the trousers will not be damaged.

RAFFLES: Blood has a tendency to splash, Captain. Anyway I am not a good marksman. Off with your trousers, please.

> *Von Blixen miserably obeys. He is wearing long combinations.*

RAFFLES: Were your combinations hired too at Moss Bros.?

VON BLIXEN: (*gloomily*) They are my own.

RAFFLES: When you've spread the papers, Captain Petrovitch—a double thickness, please, blood soaks so—take the Captain's clothes and lay them safely in the bedroom. There's a little mud on the trousers, but we will have them cleaned before we return them to Moss Bros.

> *Bunny busies himself.*

RAFFLES: You won't reconsider giving your word, Captain?

VON BLIXEN: *Nein.*

PRINCE: A brave man, Mr. Raffles, even if absurd.

RAFFLES: We all look absurd, sir, when we are reduced to combinations.

VON BLIXEN: I will protest with my dying breath that in civilised countries one agent does not kill another agent. An agent is always exchanged.

RAFFLES: (*to the Prince*) Perhaps after all, sir, killing is not strictly necessary. An officer of the Prussian Hussars can hardly bicycle to Boxmoor in his combinations.

A loud knock on the outer door.

BUNNY: Come in, whoever you are.

Smith, the Albany porter, enters, eloquently the worse for Spanish wine, though for a long moment he is flabbergasted and silent at the sight of von Blixen in his combinations.

BUNNY: Well, Smith, what is it?

SMITH: I don't know, sir, what Betteridge would have done in my place. Anything unusual, he said, you report it. First I have someone who looks like His Royal Highness asking to be let in . . .

PRINCE: Yes, porter, I'm sorry I had to shake you awake.

SMITH: It's nearly six in the morning. A man's not himself at six in the morning . . . A man can't think clearly at six in the morning. I only want to do the right thing, but there's things afoot I can't understand. I dunno what Betteridge would have done at six in the morning.

PRINCE: Perhaps Betteridge did not indulge in Spanish wine.

SMITH: It's not the Spanish wine, sir. It's them at the door with a stretcher and a corpse demanding to be let in. It's not what we are accustomed to at Albany. No dogs, no cats, no women—that's the rule. But what about a corpse, sir, I ask you?

RAFFLES: Is it a woman's corpse?

SMITH: No, sir, a man's as far as I can make out from the boots—which is all I can see, for the face is covered with a handkerchief.

RAFFLES: There are no rules against admitting a *man's* corpse, are there, Bunny?

BUNNY: Don't ask me. I give up. I give up.

SMITH: Do I understand I'm to let them in, sir?

BUNNY: Let them all come.

Smith goes out to open the front door.

VON BLIXEN: Please. I give in. I will promise anything. Only let me put on my trousers.

RAFFLES: Your promise comes too late, Captain. And a corpse won't care about your combinations.

All stare in suspense at the door. Inspector Mackenzie enters first backwards at one end of a ladder which is serving as a stretcher. On it, the body covered with an overcoat and the face with a handkerchief, lies the body of the Marquess of Queensberry. Guiding the other end is Lord Alfred Douglas. Raffles removes the handkerchief. The Prince and Bunny come and look down at the Marquess.

Nothing in his life became him like the leaving of it. (*He puts back the handkerchief.*)

PRINCE: Is he dead?

INSPECTOR: He hasna moved since he fell, sir, but for one wee twitch i' the right leg.

PRINCE: He will be mourned by the boxing profession. I don't know who else.

BUNNY: I suppose we ought to get an ambulance.

LORD ALFRED: No hurry, Bunny. If he's dead it's too late, and if he's dying we don't want to *encourage* life, do we?

"Oh let him pass; he hates him
That would upon the rack of this tough world
Stretch him out longer."

PRINCE: All the same, Lord Alfred . . . Porter, which is the nearest hospital?

SMITH: I'd say, Your Royal Highness, it would be the St. James's Hospital for Diseases of the Skin round the corner in Soho.

PRINCE: I suppose they'd have an ambulance?

SMITH: I couldn't be sure, sir, they deal more with walking cases.

RAFFLES: Try them anyway on your telephone.

Smith leaves.

Bunny and I don't want to spend what's left of the night with a dead marquess. It would spoil our breakfast.

INSPECTOR: Neither of you will take your breakfast here, sir. We'll serve you that at the Yard.

RAFFLES: No, no. I must refuse your invitation, Inspector. The Yard as a restaurant doesn't attract me. Bunny and I are going to have a little race down the Ropewalk, and you are blocking our way.

Raffles raises the revolver.

INSPECTOR: You are only bluffing, Raffles. The safety catch is on.

RAFFLES: (*clicking it off*) Thank you for reminding me.

INSPECTOR: You are still bluffing. I ken my man, Raffles. I've been at your heels a long time like a faithful dog. You are not the killing type.

RAFFLES: Oh, but I've changed, Inspector. In South Africa they taught me to kill. Even dogs when food was short.

INSPECTOR: Be a sensible laddie. Give me that gun, and I promise to speak up for you at the trial like I spoke up for your friend.

RAFFLES: No, Mackenzie. I've always said I prefer a rope and a quick drop to a long dull old age. Get away from the door. There are many men I'd much rather shoot than you.

INSPECTOR: I tell you—give me that gun.

Raffles raises it and Mackenzie doesn't move. Raffles hesitates and then tosses the gun to the floor at Mackenzie's feet.

RAFFLES: You win, Mackenzie. Bring out your bracelets. If only you'd been in uniform—but I can't bear spoiling those bloody tweeds of yours.

PRINCE: Excuse me interrupting a rather personal scene. My knowledge of the law is limited. But on what charge are you arresting him?

INSPECTOR: Why, for one, sir, stealing that gold box there.

PRINCE: My box. And I make no charge.

INSPECTOR: There remains, sir, a matter of five hundred sovereigns.

RAFFLES: Minus twelve, and all you recovered from my pockets.

LORD ALFRED: Mr. Raffles at my request was recovering a debt. They were the allowance that dead monster owed me.

INSPECTOR: Ye should learn, ma lord, to spik wi' more respect of the departed. When he slipped on the roof up there and crashed through the glass, he offered up a prayer to the Almighty. Whatever his sins it will not ha' gone unheard.

LORD ALFRED: What did he say?

INSPECTOR: He said "My God," my lord. (*The Inspector blows his nose loudly.*)

PRINCE: Well, Inspector, there seems little we can do against Mr. Raffles.

INSPECTOR: There are still the letters, sir.

PRINCE: They were not stolen by these gentlemen. On the contrary they saved them from the hands of a foreign agent sent by my nephew, the Emperor of Germany. That fellow there in combinations.

INSPECTOR: (*with mounting irritation*) At least you'll let me arrest *him*, sir?

PRINCE: I think you would find difficulty in proving anything. There are no letters on him, and you have no warrant. Better consult your friend in the Special Branch. I think he will want to exchange him—or to turn him. Isn't that the correct expression, Captain?

VON BLIXEN: I am not one who can be turned, Your Royal Highness.

PRINCE: Bravo.

INSPECTOR: Are all the letters recovered, sir?

PRINCE: Not all. Quite a number must be blowing about the High Street of Boxmoor. Don't worry. Alice is a common name—and so, I'm afraid, is Bertie. Let us hope they don't lead to any misunderstandings among the inhabitants of Boxmoor.

VON BLIXEN: Your Royal Highness, would you allow me to put on my trousers? I feel a cold coming on. (*He sneezes.*)

PRINCE: Probably caught from Inspector Mackenzie.

BUNNY: Go and take a pin, Captain.

Von Blixen goes towards the bedroom. He pauses in the doorway.

VON BLIXEN: Herr Raffles, I will admit to you now what I could not admit under the threat of death. I would not be able to return to Boxmoor. Your bicycle has a puncture in both tyres. English tyres, of course.

He goes.

PRINCE: We seem at last to be reaching what I have always desired in politics, a peaceful understanding.

RAFFLES: We owe it to you, sir.

PRINCE: Don't feel downhearted, Inspector. We owe it also to your tact and diplomatic sense. I think I have never enjoyed a long night more. Now I look forward to a little breakfast at Marlborough House—some kidneys and bacon, a well-done steak, and a pint of claret. Then I can face the humdrum world again. I would invite you, gentlemen, to join me, but you have a corpse to guard, and you, Inspector, will no doubt wish to return to Scotland Yard. You will have a rather complicated report to write, but I'm sure you will do it with all the finesse for which your countrymen are famous.

INSPECTOR: But, sir, what about the foreign agent?

PRINCE: Oh, leave him to the Special Branch. I have little doubt he can claim diplomatic immunity.

INSPECTOR: He may flee the country, sir.

PRINCE: Then look for him in Africa. Most of the lions are in British territory.

INSPECTOR: And the deceased?

RAFFLES: We will see it safely delivered to the hospital.

PRINCE: Your report will not wait, Inspector.

INSPECTOR: (*unwillingly*) Then I must wish you good night, sir?

PRINCE: No, good morning, Inspector. The sun has risen.

RAFFLES: No hard feelings, Inspector?

INSPECTOR: I'll not be saying goodbye to you, Raffles.

The Inspector leaves.

LORD ALFRED: With your permission, sir, I will leave for Victoria Station and Paris. My elder brother will bury the corpse in an adequate way. I see no reason to attend the funeral.

PRINCE: No doubt you are off to your friend, Mr. Wilde?

LORD ALFRED: We may happen to run into each other, sir.

PRINCE: I don't like his tastes, but I like his plays. I will never forget that he was a good friend to an old friend of mine, Mrs. Langtry.

LORD ALFRED: Your message will hearten him, sir.

PRINCE: Just let him stay out of England. They manage these things better in France. Good-bye, Lord Alfred.

LORD ALFRED: Good-bye, sir.

PRINCE: Be careful, my boy.

Lord Alfred leaves.

And now, Mr. Raffles—I would have preferred to speak to Mr. Jones who fought at Spion Kop—I have a request to make.

RAFFLES: You have been very generous, sir. You have only to command.

PRINCE: It has been an unprofitable night for you. You have risen from the dead—unlike Lord Queensberry. Inspector Mackenzie will not forgive that. Promise me that in future England will know only Raffles, the cricketer, and not Raffles, the amateur cracksman.

RAFFLES: (*after hesitation*) Very well, I promise, sir.

PRINCE: Then good morning to you both. Look after your shoulder, Mr. Raffles. I expect to see you take the field next summer. (*He walks towards the door and turns*) Wearing a white tie, Mr. Raffles, was a bad mistake. It was time for you to retire.

RAFFLES: Sir, you have forgotten the box.

PRINCE: A present to Mr. Jones from Mr. Portland—of less value than the one he gave me.

He leaves.

RAFFLES: A great gentleman, Bunny. He'll make a great king—if the gods allow him time.

A pause. Bunny moves round the room turning out lights. The morning sun comes in.

Well, Bunny, you voted for cricket and cricket it will have to be.

BUNNY: Do you regret it very much, A.J.?

RAFFLES: There's a long penurious winter ahead.

BUNNY: At least there's the box to melt down—and the diamonds are fine ones.

RAFFLES: One doesn't sell a present like that. I shall keep my Sullivans in it—cigarettes unlike cigars don't need sandalwood.

BUNNY: Then how shall we manage, A.J.?

RAFFLES: I think a winter on the Continent is indicated, Bunny. I made no promise about the Continent. Versailles perhaps is too large for us—and a little too vulgar. We should be treading in the footsteps of so many trippers. Perhaps we might case one of the smaller chateaux of the Loire, Bunny?

BUNNY: You were never much good at French, A.J.

RAFFLES: True, but I rather fancy my American accent. American visitors are very welcome on the Loire. There's always a needy chateau in search of a rich marriage. I could be one of the obscurer Rockefellers.

Von Blixen enters dressed again as a waiter.

Ah, Captain, I hope you bear us no ill will for our little comedy.

VON BLIXEN: I am ashamed. To have been beaten by St. Petersburg.

RAFFLES: Not by St. Petersburg, Captain. By Rugby. The school not the railway junction. We are two amateurs.

VON BLIXEN: That is worse.

RAFFLES: No, no. Here in England the Gentlemen quite often beat the Players.

Smith enters with a tarpaulin over his arm.

SMITH: Sir, they've sent an ambulance. It's down in the forecourt, but the men are all dressed up in white coats an' I'm afraid to disturb some of the old ones here like Mr. Grosvenor on Staircase B. It's not pleasant if you are ninety to look out of the window an' see a corpse carried down the Ropewalk.

BUNNY: Very thoughtful of you, Smith. What do you suggest?

SMITH: Well, sir, a ladder's different to a stretcher an' if we cover the corpse with a tarpaulin it might well be some pots of paint the workmen have left behind.

RAFFLES: You are a worthy successor of Betteridge. This gentleman is leaving and I'm sure he'll lend you a hand. Please, Captain. I would not ask it if you were in the uniform of the Prussian Hussars.

VON BLIXEN: I am your prisoner. I must obey.

RAFFLES: To carry a stretcher—if it is not a military one— is not forbidden by the Geneva Convention.

> Smith spreads the tarpaulin in place of the coat. Von Blixen unwillingly takes up the end of the ladder and they begin to carry the body towards the door. Suddenly the tarpaulin is thrown aside and the Marquess sits up with a wild expression.

MARQUESS: (looking from von Blixen to Smith) Where am I? Who the devil are you?

RAFFLES: Please lie down and be quiet, Lord Queensberry. There is nothing to be alarmed about.

MARQUESS: Where are they taking me?

RAFFLES: To the St. James's Hospital, my lord, for Diseases of the Skin and Venereal Infections. Carry on, Smith.

CURTAIN